CHINESE ACCOUNT

OF

THE OPIUM WAR.

THE Manchu Annals introduce the history of the English opium war with a statement that, early in the summer of 1838, the Director of the Court of State Ceremonial, HWANG TSIOH-TSZ,[a] represented in a Memorial to the Throne that the growing consumption of foreign opium was at the root of all China's troubles. Silver,—and coined dollars proportionately, —was becoming scarce and relatively dear, the tael having advanced from 1,000 to 1,600 cash in price;[b] the revenue was in confusion, peculation rife, and trade disorganized. Opium, he said, came from England; but, though those foreigners were ready enough to weaken China and absorb her wealth by encouraging its use, so severely did they forbid smoking amongst themselves that offending ships were sunk by heavy guns. They had possessed themselves of [Koh-liu-pa or[c]] Java by this means, and had endeavoured to seduce Annam, which state,

[a] 黃爵滋

[b] DOBELL says the Spanish dollar was worth 750 cash in A.D. 1800.

[c] 葛留巴

however, had firmly discouraged any relations with them. They were now ruining the bodies and the fortunes of the Chinese with their abominable poison; and the memorialist proposed that the penalty of death should be decreed against all offenders. In consequence of this the Emperor at once remitted the matter to the consideration of all the high provincial authorities. Without a single exception, those officers recommended the most stringent measures, and he amongst them who wrote the most uncompromisingly was LIN TSÊH-SÜ,[a] Viceroy of Hu Kwang, who was at once sent for to Peking, whence, after receiving the Emperor's instructions, he was despatched as Special Imperial Commissioner to Canton, armed with full Admiral's powers in addition.

A hundred and fifty years or so earlier, opium had been admitted into China and taxed as an ordinary drug; but, previous to the year 1765, the annual import had never exceeded 200 chests. In consequence of the rapidly increasing number of smokers, the import was first forbidden in 1796. Notwithstanding this prohibition, the annual clandestine sales had, by the year 1820, reached nearly 4,000 chests. First stored at Macao, the opium gradually gravitated to Whampoa; but, after the publication of the first severe prohibitions in the "thirties," it was finally stowed in hulks lying off the Ling-ting[b]

[a] 林則徐　　[b] 伶仃

Islands, a convenient spot commanding several water-routes. The foreign ships used to deposit their opium here, and then proceed to the ports with the rest of their cargoes. The Foochow, Ningpo, and Shanghai junks imported their opium from the high seas, whilst the Canton merchants used to arrange the price in Canton, and then bring it from the hulks. At first there were only five of these hulks, and the maximum quantity of opium on board did not exceed from 4,000 to 5,000 chests, so that the whole might easily have been set on fire; but, as the Viceroy JUAN YÜAN[a] had asked for some delay, in order to devise a plan for driving the hulks away, time went on until there were as many as twenty-five hulks, and 20,000 chests of opium. This was in the year 1826, some time after the Viceroy LI HUNG-PIN[b] had established his service of cruising junks. These junks, for a monthly bribe of Tls. 36,000, allowed the opium to pass freely into port.

It had previously been the rule that no silver was to go out of the country, and that merchandise was to be exchanged for merchandise: as much bullion as $500,000 a year was brought by foreign traders to adjust the balance: but it gradually came to pass that a balance of silver had to be annually made up on the Chinese side. To remedy this, the Viceroy LU K'UN[c] abolished the cruisers altogether

[a] 阮元　　[b] 李鴻賓　　[c] 盧坤

in 1832. In 1837 the Viceroy Têng T'ing-chêng [a] re-established the cruising navy; but the Commodore Han Shao-k'ing [b] arranged with the foreign ships to convoy the opium for a percentage, which percentage he represented as being captured opium, and even undertook the import of opium himself. For these eminent services he received a peacock's feather, and was made a rear-admiral; in consequence of which the yearly import gradually reached a figure of 40,000 or 50,000 chests. The suggestion made by certain Peking officials that this opium should be regularly taxed as a drug was rejected; and in the spring of 1839 Commissioner Lin appeared upon the scene.

Lin called upon the hong merchant Ng I-wo [c] [Howqua] to deliver up Chatun [d] [Jardine] and Tinti [e] [Dent], who had been for many years in the habit of dealing in opium. Chatun, having got wind of this, had already made his escape, but Tinti came with the English Company's Consul Ilut [f] [Elliot] from Macao to the Canton Foreign Factory. Lin Tsêh-sü sent a body of soldiers to keep a watch upon them there and to surround the Líptak [g] Fort, in the Canton River, with a cordon of rafts, so as to prevent communication therewith. He then ordered the surrender, within a given date, of all the opium on

[a] 鄧廷楨　[b] 韓肇慶　[c] 伍怡和　[d] 查頓
[e] 顛池　[f] 義律　[g] 靂德

board the 25 hulks at Ling-ting, and a free pardon, failing which, he threatened to stop supplies of fuel and water, and to prevent trade. He proceeded to catechise the young gentry attached to the local university, and learnt from their unanimous testimony that the failure of the opium laws was entirely owing to the connivance of the navy. HAN SHAO-K'ING was cashiered at his recommendation; but it was impossible to punish him capitally or according to his full deserts, as the Viceroy TÊNG had recommended him for the post.

The "Company's Consul"[a] was a foreign official despatched by the King of England to superintend trading operations. Foreign traders of other nationalities looked after their own trade as individuals. England alone had a separate company, consisting of the richest merchants in the kingdom, who had subscribed a capital of $30,000,000; and the King sent this consular officer to manage the whole concern. All the holding-out for rights and the overbearing demands made upon China were the doing of this Consul. Hence the traders of the other countries were as the individual salt-dealers of China, whilst the Company was like the salt-monopolists. Their charter was first for 30 years, but was afterwards renewed for 60 years. In 1833 the Company's charter ceased to be exclusive in China, and there was no longer a

[a] 公司領事

Consul at Canton. This was the first great change in foreign affairs. When the Viceroy LU K‘UN first came to Canton, he was ignorant of our true interests, gave ear to the suggestions of the foreign traders, and sent a despatch to England directing a Consul to be sent as before. The first was LO LUTPI[a] [Lord NAPIER] who forced his ships past the Bogue, began hostilities, and was finally constrained to return home. The next was ELLIOT, who had been at Canton for three years when he was besieged in the factory as above described. Within a week or two he sent in an official petition, offering to surrender the opium as instructed, and also to send back to Canton all the opium-ships on their way to Japan. The total number of chests thus surrendered was 20,283, or, at 120 catties apiece, 2,376,000 catties of the drug. LIN TSÊH-SÜ and the Viceroy TÊNG proceeded to the Bogue to superintend the delivery, which was completed in the month of May. It was agreed to bestow three catties of tea for each one of opium, and the opium was ordered by the Emperor to be destroyed, instead of being sent to Peking as proposed,—the object being to impress the people by this public spectacle. ' This destruction was carried out at the Bogue in the presence of LIN TSÊH-SÜ, the Viceroy, and the Governor. At an elevated spot on the shore a space was barricaded in; here a pit

[a] 羅律爾

was dug, and filled with opium mixed with brine: into this, again, lime was thrown, forming a scalding furnace, which made a kind of boiling soup of the opium. In the evening the mixture was let out by sluices, and allowed to flow out to sea with the ebb tide.

Opium is of four sorts: the best is *Kung pán t'ou*[a] [or Patna]; the *Pák t'ou*[b] [or Malwa] comes next, and the *Kèm fa t'ou*[c] [*chin hwa t'u* or Persian] next again; each chest containing 40 balls. Besides these, there is a dearer sort called the smaller *Kung pán*. They all come from Bengal and [? Madras][d] in India. At the Indian auctions as many as 12,000 chests are sometimes sold in a month. Though some of this goes to countries farther south, the greater part goes to China, which takes from 50,000 to 60,000 chests a year. Its price in India is about $250 a chest, which price is more than doubled by the time it reaches Canton. Thus, the destruction of property was from $5,000,000 to $6,000,000 cost price, or over $10,000,000 including the profit. A number of traders from other countries came to witness the spectacle, and composed eulogistic essays upon the excellence of China's policy in this matter.

Commissioner LIN then issued orders for the ejection of all the opium hulks, and also of the disloyal traders at Macao, who were forbidden to tarry upon Chinese soil. Ships arriving with opium

[a] 公班土　[b] 白土　[c] 金花土　[d] 孟邁

would not be interfered with if they at once turned round and went back, and all ships entering port must give bonds agreeing that those found smuggling opium should be confiscated with their cargoes, and that the individuals concerned should be executed at once. These orders were, however, far too stringent, and, anyhow, contrary to the law which provides that " Mongols, and other persons beyond the pale of " civilization, shall be at liberty to ransom capital " offences by a fine payable in cattle." The American and other nations, however, gave the bonds required. On this, ELLIOT went down from Canton to Macao, and sent in a petition asking that a deputy might be despatched to Macao to discuss with him a set of rules under which a stop might be permanently put to the opium trade; and enlarging upon the abuses of the hulk system. He also requested that British ships might be permitted to anchor and discharge at Macao. This was the second great turning-point in foreign affairs. LIN, however, resolutely objected to this proposal, grounding his objections on the fact that twenty-five ships were the fixed number sanctioned for Macao; and that, if the British did not come to Whampoa, the Maritime Customs would have no work to do, nor would there be any means of putting a check upon opium smuggling. To this ELLIOT replied that, unless permission were granted to anchor at Macao, there would be no basis for an understanding. He declined either to receive the tea bestowed upon him, or to give bonds; and said he must await instructions from his Government before he could allow ships to enter port. ELLIOT had already sent despatches home by a trading ship, to which a reply might be expected in six months, so that a little delay would have made no difference. But in the month of July there occurred the Tsim-sha Point[a] case, in which a Chinese, named LIN WEI-HI,[b] was killed by a foreign sailor [7th July]. Orders were sent to ELLIOT to surrender the offender in satisfaction; but ELLIOT—who, however, had no intention of deliberately disobeying—only had up for examination five black barbarians, not the real criminals, whilst he offered rewards to any who should come forward as informers. In August the Commissioner LIN and the Viceroy TÊNG, in accordance with law, cut off the supply of fuel and provisions from Macao. They also held that, as the foreigners resident in Macao were there for purposes of trade, they had no right to tarry at Macao, seeing that they no longer entered port to trade. On this ELLIOT, together with his family and compatriots at Macao, fifty-seven families in all, removed from Macao, and took quarters on board the trading ships at Tsim-sha Point. ELLIOT, now being exasperated, then secretly sent for two men-of-war from the foreign ports, and, with three large

[a] 尖沙嘴 (opposite Hongkong).   [b] 林維喜

trading ships fitted up as cruisers, proceeded to Cowloon, where, under pretext of demanding food, he engaged our naval force in battle. Captain LAI EN-TSIOH[a] succeeded in sinking a two-masted foreign ship, two sampans, and a Spanish hulk hired by the British. In the eighth moon [October] ELLIOT got the Europeans at Macao to send a message for him, to the effect that he was willing to send away the hulks and the disloyal traders, and also that the trading ships were willing to give bonds agreeing to the confiscation of ship and cargo in cases of smuggling [opium]; but he objected to the words "the "individuals concerned to be executed at once." This was the third turning-point in Canton affairs. LIN TSÊH-SÜ, however, insisted upon the insertion of these words, so that the bonds of all nationalities might be alike; and, moreover, demanded the surrender of the murderer. Shortly after this, two English trading ships did sign bonds as required, but ELLIOT sent two men-of-war [the "Volage" and "Hyacinth"] after them to prevent it. He also petitioned us not to attack and destroy the ships at Tsimsha Point, so that he might await despatches from England: but Admiral KWAN T'IEN-P'EI[b] returned his petition because the murderer was not given up. During these premises, five of our war-ships went to preserve order on the sea-board, and, the petition

[a] 賴 恩 爵   [b] 關 天 培

having been rejected, the English mistook our red flags for a declaration of war, and opened fire;—for in Europe a red flag means war, and a white one peace. Admiral Kwan returned their fire, and knocked the figure-head off one ship, causing the death by drowning of many European soldiers. In November they next unsuccessfully attacked our fort north of Tsim-sha Point; but, as we had poisoned the wells, and they feared a night attack, they made off to their ships again.

On receipt of the news of the Cowloon affair, the Emperor wrote on the memorialists' report:—" I do " not fear your rashness, gentlemen, so much as I fear " your cowardice." The Imperial Edict of the 8th of the 11th moon (December) ran:—"The English, ever " since the opium interdiction, have been vacillating " in their conduct. It is no longer consistent with " dignity to continue to permit their trade. The " trifle of customs duties is of no importance to us. " Our dynasty, in conciliating foreigners, has shewn " kindness exceeding deep; but the English, instead " of being grateful for this, have indulged in ferocious " violence, so that they are in the wrong whilst we in " the right, as all the world must know. As they have " placed themselves outside the pale of our favour, " they are not entitled to pity. Let, therefore, the " English trade be at once stopped." In the original memorial there was a proposal that those ships which obeyed the law should receive protection, whilst those which were recalcitrant should suffer by being repelled, on which the Emperor wrote:—"They are all men "of the same country: if they are dealt with "differently, there must be inconsistency in it." The above is the history of the cutting-off of English trade, owing to the opium prohibition.

Meanwhile, one TSÊNG WANG-YEN,[a] Director of the Revision Court, had recommended the Emperor to close the Customs Houses, and put a complete stop to sea-going trade with all countries. This suggestion was referred to Commissioner LIN, who strongly objected to it, arguing that, if those who had not broken the prohibition were excluded from trade without reason, they would join in a general attack upon us. The matter then dropped.

After the closing of the ports to the English, from twenty to thirty ships arrived, none of which were allowed to enter, much to the chagrin of everybody. ELLIOT now sent in a second petition, saying that he had served some years at Canton, and was really desirous of peace; that he was very much distressed at the confusion into which affairs had drifted; that he would be very pleased to act in obedience to the laws of the Great Pure Dynasty, so long as he had not to break his own country's laws: and he begged that his countrymen might be allowed to return to

[a] 曾望顏

Macao pending the arrival of instructions from home, when trade could be re-opened. This is the fourth turning-point in Canton affairs.

Lin Tsêh-sü held, however, in view of the Emperor's recent instructions, that any divergence therefrom was inexpedient, and therefore repeated the interdiction in the strongest terms. Over ten ships then weighed anchor and went out to Ló-mán Shan,[a] where, in company with a number of new arrivals, they gave opium in exchange for provisions brought to them by the fishing boats. Lin Tsêh-sü was now made Viceroy, and arranged with Admiral Kwan a plan for utilizing the *tanka* boatmen and fishing-craft in an attack upon the disloyal junks, the Chinese war-junks being unfitted for the high seas. A number of boats were disposed in the various creeks and inlets, and it was arranged that an attack should be made simultaneously from four directions, going out and returning on one tide. Twenty-three junks, engaged in exchanging supplies for opium, were burnt at Ch'ang-sha Wan,[b] in the month of March, a number of disloyal Chinese were burnt in their huts on shore, or drowned; and a dozen or so were taken prisoners. The foreign ships hurriedly moved off to escape the fire-boats. The eighteen months' law condemning opium-smokers to strangulation, and opium-dealers to decapitation had now been in

[a] 老萬山　　[b] 長沙灣

force the best part of a year, and as the watch kept all over the Empire was very strict, over half the smokers were already cured. Meantime, the news of the stoppage of trade reached England, and no one would sell the stocks of tea at the various emporia, which thus accumulated until famine prices were reached, so that during this time a profitable trade was done by Canton and Foochow junks with Singapore and other places in the south. There was no silver available in the capital of London, where the merchants were obliged to borrow large sums from neighbouring emporia in order to meet their engagements. ELLIOT had sent home for troops, and the Queen directed Parliament to deliberate upon the matter. The official body, civil and military, were for war, whilst the mercantile interest was for peace. Discussion went on for several days without any definite result, and at last lots were drawn in the Lo Chan-sz Temple[a] [? division before the Lord Chancellor] and three tickets were found in favour of war, which was therefore decided upon. The Queen ordered her relative by marriage, PEH-MEH,[b] [Sir GORDON BREMER] to take a dozen or so of warships under his command, to which were added twenty or thirty guard-ships from India. This was reported to the Throne by LIN TSÊH-SÜ in the month of June; but the Emperor still said:—"What can they do if

[a] 羅占士神廟   [b] 伯麥

" we quietly wait on the defensive and watch their
" movements?" During the night of the 9th of the
fifth moon [some time in June] LIN TSÊH-SÜ sent
another naval force to the sea-board off Mo-tau,[a]
and succeeded in burning with his fireships two
foreign sampans, besides killing four white foreigners;
and one large foreign ship was obliged to escape the
fire by leaving its anchor behind. Eleven fishing
boats were burnt, and thirteen traitorous Chinese
taken prisoners. Towards the end of June, fifteen
British men-of-war, including three steamers, assem-
bled at the Cum-sing Moon,[b] the rest remaining at
Ló-mán Shan. LIN TSÊH-SÜ sent down ten fireships in
pairs, each pair connected by iron chains, which swept
down thus with the tide. The foreign ships all made
off hastily: but two sampans were burnt; and from
this time the English did not venture again into port.

From the time of his arrival in Canton, LIN
TSÊH-SÜ had sent out spies daily to get foreign
information, and to translate European works. He
had also purchased newspapers, and discovered therefrom that the Europeans held the Chinese navy in the
utmost contempt, but were in great dread of our
pirates and fishermen. He therefore engaged 5,000
sturdy men at $6 a month, with $6 extra for each of
their families, which sum was defrayed by subscription
amongst the members of the co-hong, the salt-dealers,

[a] 磨刀   [b] 金星門

and the Swatow merchants. He also extended a chain barrier and a system of rafts across the Bogue, and set up on both banks over 200 guns which he had purchased from the different European countries. He further hired sixty boats of various sorts, which he equipped for fighting, and also prepared 20 fireships and over 100 smaller boats to attack the foreign ships. Besides all this, he purchased an old foreign ship, and practised his men in the art of taking her by assault from the windward with the neap tides in their favour. Lin Tsêh-sü reviewed his fleet in person, and offered $200 for each white man, with half the amount for each black man killed. For Elliot's head $20,000 was offered, with graduated amounts, according to rank, for those of the military officers under him. Every man-of-war captured would be prize to the captors, with the exception of the arms and ammunition, which would be surrendered to the viceregal government. The result of this action was, that the traitorous Chinese became objects of suspicion to the English, and were all sent away. The river inlets west of Macao and east of the Bogue were guarded by strong detachments of troops; and, as all the other passages were too rocky and shallow for the foreign ships, they went cruising along the coasts of China. Thirty-one of them appeared off the Chê Kiang coasts, and five made an attack upon Amoy, but one of the largest [? the

" Blonde "] was sunk through the dispositions of the Viceroy Têng T'ing-chêng [transferred to Foochow on the 6th of February]. He also shipped a number of braves on board trading junks, and attacked the foreign ships at Namoa. For want of wind, these latter were unable to get away, and, having no guns astern, were unable with rifles alone to injure our junks, protected as they were with bullet-proof mantlets of hide. We damaged their sterns, and treated them to a volley of stink-pots and fire-balls, killing several dozen of the barbarian soldiers. [The " Hellas " was attacked on the 22nd of May while becalmed, and all her hands were wounded.] On the wind getting up, the barbarian ships managed to escape. In the sixth moon [5th July 1840] their whole fleet attacked and captured Ting-hai [Chusan] and blockading detachments then swept the coasts of Fu Kien and Kwang Tung. A month later the foreign ships made a sudden attack upon the neck of land behind Macao, but several of their small boats were sunk by our guns, and a score or more of their eyes [officers] and men were wounded. A month later Lin Tsêh-sü, observing a squadron of five ships [" Enterprise," " Larne," " Louisa," " Hyacinth "] off Mo-tau, under Smith's[a] command, sent five junks to sea to annihilate them, each junk carrying 600 men. Captain Ma Ch'ên[b] happened to engage [Commodore]

[a] 士密　　　[b] 馬辰

SMITH's ship first, and succeeded in damaging her bows, so that she reeled over, and some marines were drowned. For a long time we surrounded her, until all her ammunition was fired off; but the other ships sent a dozen or so of boats to surround MA CH'ÊN's junk, and, whilst MA CH'ÊN was engaged with these, SMITH's ship managed to escape. We picked up several corpses, and captured some arms and a flag: the facts were duly reported to the Emperor, who said LIN "had caused the "war by his excessive zeal, and had killed people "in order to close their mouths." The meaning of this was that the Chê Kiang authorities were totally unable to do anything for the recovery of Ting-hai, and there was no possibility of anyone doing so except by fighting at sea, at which exercise the foreign ships excelled us; whilst it had been whispered to the Emperor that the foreigners might take advantage of China's unreadiness for war to invade the country. The Emperor had also now heard that, before the opium was surrendered, a promise, since broken, had been made to pay for it, which was the cause of hostilities: others told him that the Viceroy TÊNG's report of the Amoy affair was untrue. ILIPU,[a] Viceroy at Nanking, was therefore sent as Imperial Commissioner to Ningpo, and orders were sent to all the Governors of the Coast

[a] 伊里布

Provinces to receive at once and report to the Emperor the contents of any letters handed in by foreign ships. The Under Secretaries Hwang Tsioh-tsz and K'ɪ Tsun-tsao[a] were sent to observe the course of events in Fu Kien Province. In the month of August, the foreign chief Bremer and five ships arrived at Tientsin, with letters from the Pa-li-man[b] office [Parliament] addressed to the "Premier of the "Great Pure Dynasty," and containing a number of categorical demands. First, he demanded the value of "the produce" (as the first letters euphoniously styled "opium"), or "opium" (as he afterwards plainly called it). Secondly, he demanded that Canton, Amoy, Foochow, Ting-hai, and Shanghai should be opened to trade. Thirdly, terms of equality. Fourthly, a war indemnity. Fifthly, that merchants on shore must not be held responsible for the doings of opium-ships on the seas. Sixthly, the abolition of the co-hong monopoly. These demands were referred to Peking by K'ɪshen,[c] Viceroy of Chih Li, and meanwhile the foreign ships had not come north, as it was hoped that the negotiations for commercial privileges would be successful; so that, if things had been properly managed, the treaty would have been concluded on the spot. The Tientsin *taotai* Luh Kien-ying[d] represented that the three first demands were the most important, and suggested that the opium

[a] 祁雋藻　[b] 巴釐滿衙門　[c] 琦善　[d] 陸建瀛

should be paid for by remission of duties; that Macao should be an open port; and that the Hoppo be placed on terms of equality with them; but that, adhering to the principle of rigidly excluding opium, these concessions should be conditional upon opium not coming; and that the abolition of the co-hong question should be referred by them to LIN TSÊH-SÜ at Canton. In this way satisfaction would be given without compromising China's dignity. This is the fifth turning-point in western affairs. However, those charged with the negotiations thought that they would not gain so much credit by concluding an arrangement at once at Tientsin as if they magnified and dragged on the negotiations; and therefore they would give no decided answers to any of the demands. Moreover, in the reply, it was hinted that LIN TSÊH-SÜ would be severely punished if it were found by the Emperor's Commissioner that there was anything crooked in the alleged "delivery-up of the opium" promise of last year. An Imperial edict appointed K'ISHEN as Commissioner to enquire into the matter. LIN TSÊH-SÜ and TÊNG T'ING-CHÊNG were degraded, but ordered to await the result of investigation at Canton. Orders were also given to all the coast authorities not to fire upon the European ships. The applicants then left Tientsin, and declined to surrender Ting-hai, on the ground that the Chinese Government would give no decided answer. Half of their naval force left Chusan for Canton. Lin Tsêh-sü had represented meanwhile that the other nationalities were very indignant at the prolonged stoppage of trade by the British, and had said that they would send home for armed forces of their own if the English did not return quickly. This, he said, was just what we wanted,—to set one enemy against the other. Three million taels would buy all the ships and guns that China wanted; and, by thus imitating the enemy's best methods, we should be able to constrain him with his own weapons, and allow him to wear himself out in seeking to attack us. He offered to redeem his past errors by proceeding to Chê Kiang with a view to recovering Ting-hai. The Emperor, however, would not agree to his proposals. In November Elliot returned to Chê Kiang, and had an interview with Ilipu at Chên-hai. He demanded the surrender of the captured chief An-t'u-tê[a] [Captain Anstruther]; and also of the foreign ship ["Kite"] which had been stranded on a sandbank off Ningpo in September, together with a score or two of white and black barbarians. He left unsuccessful. Ilipu after this sent his slave Chang-hi[b] to the foreign ships with a present of beef and wine, and the "welcome news" of the degradation of Lin and Têng. The foreign chief Bremer shook his head, and said:—"Mr. Lin is one of China's best

[a] 安突德　　　[b] 張喜

"Viceroys, and an able and plucky man, though he does not understand foreign ways. You can stop the opium trade, but you cannot stop *all* our trade, for, if you do that, you will stop our means of subsistence; and we must struggle for trading privileges with all our might. You are very wrong if you think we have come here out of any feeling of hostility towards the Viceroy LIN." Meanwhile the people of Chih Li and Shan Tung vied with each other in their representations of the modest character of the enemy; in consequence of which T'OHUNPU,[a] Governor of Shan Tung, sent presents to the foreign fleet, and then represented to the Emperor that the foreigners had come ashore and made obeisance in a body! At the same time the new Viceroy, ILIANG,[b] reported that half of our fleet which had been thrown out of commission at Canton, had fallen into the enemy's hands. In November K'ISHEN arrived in Canton; and, finding the official despatches from ELLIOT surrendering the opium, tried to find faults in LIN's conduct; but was unsuccessful. He then lost the good-will of the military by proposing to execute the captain who, as he made out, had provoked the naval engagement by firing the first shot. The consequence of this was that a number of Chinese braves were discharged and went over to the English; nay, even received posts

[a] 託渾布   [b] 怡良

of trust from them. The sunken piles were removed from the river at Wáng-tong,[a] and several interviews were had with ELLIOT at the Bogue, in consequence of which the foreign ships were able to survey the river and make charts, not to mention finding out all about our dispositions. On the advice of the Salt Comptroller WANG TUH,[b] the services of all the civil and military officials were dispensed with, and communications were entrusted entirely to a wretched Chinese traitor named PAO P'ÊNG,[c] who had once been the pet boy of the traitor DENT, and whom ELLIOT regarded as a menial, conceiving thereupon a greater contempt for China's resources in men than ever. ELLIOT wrote to K'ISHEN, "If you increase "the number of your soldiers against us, I will not "consent to peace;" and the result was that we dared not re-engage the discharged men. Whenever the traitorous spies were denounced, the denouncers were accused of being spies; and whenever persons offered information about the foreigners, they were told:— "I am not like Viceroy LIN, who, as one of China's "great officers, kept spying upon the foreigners all "day." In short, the whole policy of the former incumbents was reversed. Perhaps the idea in all this was to captivate the foreign mind; but the real fact was that the enemy was manufacturing a still larger number of boats and junks of all shapes and

[a] 橫擋   [b] 王篤   [c] 鮑鵬

sizes, besides engaging opium-running snake-boats, etc., all armed with rockets, stink-pots, ladders, and every kind of equipment. Admiral KWAN confidentially recommended an increase of troops; but K'ISHEN firmly refused, fearing that this would jeopardise the peace negotiations. Notwithstanding an indemnity of seven million taels offered by him for the opium destroyed, a port was also demanded. K'ISHEN at first thought of Amoy and Hongkong, and consulted TÊNG T'ING-CHÊNG; but the latter objected to Amoy as being the key to Fu Kien; and, as to Hongkong, he argued that this island occupied a prominent and central position in Canton waters, sheltered from bad weather by the two islands of Tsimshá Tsui[a] and K'wên-tái Lou,[b] which, if fortified by the English, would be a perpetual menace to Canton. K'ISHEN had represented this to the Throne, and therefore could not go back upon his own word, and accept ELLIOT's proposals. Correspondence and interviews led to no result; so at last ELLIOT, on the 7th of January 1841, suddenly attacked the Shá-kok[c] and the Tái-kok[d] forts,—the first important line of defence outside the Bogue. The guns of the fleet bombarded the forts in front, and about 2,000 Chinese traitors scaled the hills and attacked them in the rear. A hundred or more of these were blown up by exploded mines; but the rest, far out-

[a] 尖沙嘴 [b] 裙帶路 [c] 沙角 [d] 大角

numbering the garrison of 600 men, came swarming up notwithstanding. Two or three hundred more were killed by our gingalls; but at last our powder was exhausted, and the steam-launches got round to Sám-mun Hau,*a* and burnt our fleet, the crews of which either decamped or perished. The Wáng-tong, Tsing-yün and Wai-yün forts only just managed to escape destruction themselves, and were unable to offer any succour. The commandant at Tái-kok, CH'ÊN LIEN-SHÊNG,*b* and his son were killed, and the two forts fell into the rebels' hands. The other three forts, commanded by Admiral KWAN, Rear-Admiral LI T'ING-YÜ,*c* and Captain MA CH'ÊN had only a few hundred men in them, who could do nothing but regard each other with weeping eyes. Admiral KWAN sent LI to Canton to crave more troops, in which request he was supported by the whole official body; but K'ISHEN was obdurate, and simply spent the night in writing out further peace proposals, which he sent by PAO P'ÊNG to ELLIOT. Hongkong was offered in addition to the opium indemnity, and the Chê Kiang [? "Kite"] prisoners were exchanged for Ting-hai. A treaty was made, and K'ISHEN gave a dinner to ELLIOT of the Bogue. On the 11th of February the Emperor's refusal to ratify was received, and everything was upset again.

a 三門口   *b* 陳連升   *c* 李廷鈺

Now, when K'ISHEN took leave of the Emperor, he had already been instructed to grant free trade, if that should be all the English asked; but, if their demands were exorbitant, he was to keep them in good humour, strengthen his defences, and ask for reinforcements: but he was never told to discharge his men and secure peace at all costs. The Emperor was furious when he heard of the capture of the forts and the menacing attitude of the rebels, and said he would not give a cent for the opium nor yield an inch of territory. Troops from the south-western provinces were ordered to Canton, and both LIN and TÊNG were ordered to associate themselves with K'ISHEN. K'ISHEN, however, would not consult LIN upon any matter; and, though the peace negotiations had fallen through, he would not allow Admiral KWAN to strengthen himself with more troops. On the other hand, the enemy enrolled more men than ever, added to their equipments, and became a hundred times more ferocious than before. Early in February, the Emperor had launched a decree descanting upon the crimes of the rebels, and ordering the Imperial Clansman YIKSHAN[a] to Canton as Rebel Quelling Generalissimo. YANG FANG,[b] General of Hu Nan Province, and LUNGWÊN,[c] President of the Board of Revenue, were associated with him as advisers. K'IKUNG,[d] President of the Board of

[a] 奕山 [b] 楊芳 [c] 隆文 [d] 祁㯖

Punishments, was ordered to Kiang Si Province to be in charge of the Commissariat. General FANG arrived, after audience, in March; but the English had already taken the Wáng-tong and Bogue forts on the 5th of the 2nd Moon [the 26th February], when Admiral KWAN was killed. Over 300 guns, together with the 200 or more of foreign guns purchased by LIN, had fallen into the enemy's hands. The thousand or so of men newly arrived from Hu Nan were at once sent by K'ISHEN to the front. The Cantonese fled the moment the engagement began; but the Hu Nan men fought as they retreated, and half of them were drowned, together with their Commander SIANGFUH.[a] There were only two places on the Canton River narrow enough to be defended, namely, Líptak and Ishámei[b] (20 *li*) by the east channel, and Tái-wong Káo[c] (15 *li*) by the south-west. YANG FANG sent Brigadier TWAN YUNG-FUH[d] with 1,000 men to occupy a temple, about three miles distant south-east from Canton, and two miles inland from the river. Another Brigadier, CH'ANG CH'UN,[e] was sent to occupy Phœnix Hill, about two miles behind Tái-wong Káo. In neither case were measures taken sufficient to stop the ships. At Líptak and Ishámei, though junks filled with stones had been sunk, there were no soldiers to prevent the ships from removing them. The English

[a] 祥福 [b] 二沙尾 [c] 大黃滘 [d] 段永福 [e] 長春

were at first rather awed at YANG's military reputation, and, not knowing what our dispositions were, sent some white foreigners to Phœnix Hill with peace proposals. Some traitorous Chinese were with them, and they took soundings as they came. CH'ANG CH'UN sent the letter on to Canton, and meanwhile allowed the traitors to show the foreigners all over the camp; when, of course, they reported that there were no defences, and advanced, capturing Phœnix Hill and the forts commanding Líptak and Ishámei. Meanwhile K'ISHEN was deprived of his titles and honours, and the Emperor was rendered more furious than ever at receiving from ILIANG an English "proclamation," posted at Hongkong [1st February 1841], saying:—"As ye are now subjects "of Great England, ye ought in right to obey her." K'ISHEN's family was subjected to a domiciliary visit, and he himself [12th March] was haled in chains to Peking. The English, perceiving the Emperor's rage, and seeing the pass things had come to, feared that peace was farther off than ever, and were most anxious for trade, in order that they might recoup themselves the great expense of the war: besides, the other countries blamed them for keeping the trade closed for so long. They therefore sent a letter by the American head-man and HOWQUA, saying:—"If you want peace, and do not press "other matters, all we ask is trade as before; and "any ships smuggling opium may be confiscated with "their cargoes:" *i.e.* they dared not ask for either the opium indemnity or for Hongkong, as had been promised to them by K'ISHEN. YANG FANG ordered them back out of the Bogue; to which ELLIOT replied:—"The ships will retire when the Decree "authorizing trade is received;"—which was duly reported to the Throne by ILIANG and YANG FANG.

The enemy was now at our gates; our soldiers were routed, the people flying, and we had no arms; and so there was no other way of obtaining a truce and the retirement of the enemy but by temporarily giving way: and, as neither the opium indemnity nor a port was demanded, China could have done so with much better grace than before K'ISHEN's degradation. This is the sixth turning-point in Canton affairs.

YANG FANG, on his way to Canton, had heard that peace was likely to be made; so that, in order to back up K'ISHEN in anticipation, and secure his own position, he had separately recommended to the Emperor that a "haven for stowage should be granted," which proposal had considerably shaken the Emperor's confidence in him. And now, as he did not take the ground in his reports that the pirates had since been admitted, that he had been defeated, and that some compromise was necessary to get rid of the foe; nor the ground that the foreigners were by this time awe-stricken, that China's dignity had been vindicated, and that affairs had taken a turn of such importance that further mistakes should be avoided; nor, again, that defensive preparations were now complete, and extermination would at once follow further outrages; but simply indulged in empty and equivocal vapourings; the Emperor put him down as an unsoldierly, undiplomatic individual, and would not agree to his recommendations.

By this time the Ting-hai fleet had come, making a total of fifty large ships, half at Hongkong, and half in the river; and flags stuck up in the boats advertised opium for sale all along the river. YIKSHAN remained a while on the Kwang Tung frontier whilst means of attack were being hurried up from the provinces. He, LUNGWÊN, and the new Viceroy K'IKUNG, arrived in Canton on the 14th of April. YIKSHAN consulted YANG FANG and LIN TSÊH-SÜ as to what was to be done, and they both said that Canton was entirely defenceless, and that the only thing was to get the foreign ships by some ruse or other outside Líptak and Tái Wong-káo, and then work day and night to block up the river, fortify the banks, and station bodies of soldiers at suitable places, so as to avoid being at the mercy of the western men. After re-inforcing and equipping ourselves we could then (they said) resume the offensive, and seize the first favourable opportunity of wind and tide to attack and burn the fleet. This month, however, Lin Tsêh-sü received orders to proceed to Chê Kiang, the Emperor having now formed changed ideas of the respective merits both of him and of K'ishen from the reports received from the Nanking and Foochow authorities; and Yük'ien,[a] Viceroy at Nanking, was ordered to replace Ilipu as Commissioner.

At first Yikshan was sensible enough to listen to Yang Fang's advice and not risk a second fight until the new forces should have arrived; but, yielding to a desire for glory, he at last secretly ordered a sudden night attack upon the fleet from three different quarters, and only informed Yang Fang when the men had actually left the city. Yang Fang stamped and swore; but it was too late. The attack was made by 400 braves from Sz Ch'wan and by 300 Cantonese, who, at a signal from a gun, rushed on the fleet in fire-boats carrying stink-pots, fire-balls, and long boarding-pikes. A certain amount of injury was done to two ships, and five sampans and several hundred foreign soldiers were drowned. Elliot managed to effect his escape from the factory where he was, and after his departure the place was completely rifled by the Hu Nan and Sz Ch'wan soldiery. Several Americans were wounded by mistake. At daylight the fleet made a movement up to Canton, and all the combustible material, which

[a] 裕謙

had been brought down at such expense from Kwang Si, was set on fire by the steam-launches of the enemy and by the Chinese traitors. Three days later ELLIOT handed in a missive saying that a general attack would take place the next morning; and next day the city was attacked from the three sides which were surrounded by water. The 8,000 catty [five-ton] guns, which had been newly cast at Fatshan, were much dreaded by the foreigners; but, unfortunately, no suitable positions could be found for aiming them, either on shore or afloat. Our soldiers, who had been detached, regardless of what Province they came from, in such a way that men and officers were strangers to each other, broke and fled, indulged in mutual recriminations, and began to complain about their pay. K'IKUNG, moreover, was too stingy to allow more than one tent to fifteen men; so that the troops were all huddled together without discipline, and looted around just as they liked. Add to this, YIKSHAN had disposed the greater part of his forces so as to defend the south and east sides, the mud rampart behind the city to the north-west being left undefended, so that the heights were taken in one day. These consisted of the T'ien-tsz Fort under TWAN YUNG FUH, with 8,000 catty guns,—which were spiked before they had a chance of firing; the mud rampart under Captains TAI CH'ANG[a] and

[a] 岱昌

LIU TA-CHUNG;[a] and the Square Fort under CH'ANG CH'UN, which last commanded a view of the whole city, and had resisted the Manchus for six whole months when they invested Canton 200 years ago, and the capture of which enabled them at last to take the city. It ought to have been razed long ago, and all approaches to the hill should have been obstructed. But, again, as it is three miles away from the river, and full of crags, one single man might have done *something* to defend it; yet, after the mud rampart had fallen, the enemy worked round northeast without meeting with any opposition whatever. Only 100 or so of them had appeared at the foot, when the garrison of the fort made off helter-skelter, several being killed by falls in their hurry; so that this important position fell into the foreigners' hands without a struggle, and was speedily fortified by them so as to dominate the helpless city; which they proceeded to bombard. On the seventh day the Tartar-General and his advisers took refuge in the Governor's palace from the missiles which came raining down on the south-east quarter of the inner or Tartar city, and, after a consultation, sent the prefect[b] of Canton outside to propose terms. ELLIOT promptly demanded, in addition to the opium-money, a war indemnity of $6,000,000,—the question of Hongkong to remain for discussion. The money was to be paid within five

[a] 劉大忠　　[b] 余保純

days, and the ships were to retire beyond the Bogue as soon as the Tartar-General and the soldiers from other provinces should have quitted Canton. [The total British losses were seventy killed and wounded.] All this was acceded to; white flags were exhibited on the city walls; the hong merchants were ordered to furnish $2,000,000, and the rest was contributed by the Treasurer's, Salt Commissioner's, and Hoppo's chests. This was reported to the Throne,—omitting all reference to the opium and Hongkong. The foreign soldiers in Square Fort then rejoined the ships, and ELLIOT insisted on the Tartar-General and his advisers leaving the city. Accordingly YIKSHAN and LUNGWÊN retired with their troops to Kin Shan [Cumshan], a dozen miles or so from the river, and withdrew the Hu Nan troops; but YANG FANG was left in Canton to maintain order. LUNGWÊN died of shame and mortification shortly after his arrival at Cumshan.

Now, on their first arrival in Canton, the Tartar-General and his advisers had represented to the Throne that all the Cantonese people were disloyal, and all the Cantonese soldiers marauders, and therefore marines had been brought all the way from Fu Kien, to the exclusion of Cantonese: disloyal persons detected were executed without trial; and thus the Cantonese people suffered from a feeling of injustice. On the other hand, the English did not kill the

Cantonese, and always released any local braves which they had taken prisoners, occasionally even attacking parties of bandits, and prohibiting all looting, so as to gain the people's sympathies. Consequently no response was made to the offers of reward for the enemies' heads. The people had witnessed the attack upon Canton from the walls; and, when several of the city volunteers were unjustly killed by the Hu Nan braves, the former rushed, to the number of several hundred, into the Examination Hall to take revenge, and drove the soldiers helter-skelter to the Tartar-General's palace. Here they were somewhat pacified by Brigadier TWAN's being deprived of his button and feather on the spot. The foreign soldiers also earned the ill-will of the people by giving way to plundering and lust; and as 1,500 of their number did this the day after the peace, on their way down from Square Fort to the Mud Rampart, the exasperated villagers of Sám-yün[a] surrounded and killed 200 of them, including their General, PEHMEH HAPIH,[b] whose head was as large as a bucket, and whose bâton, orders, and double-barrelled pistol were also taken. The villagers of Sám-shán[c] attacked and killed another hundred of

[a] 三元里

[b] 伯麥霞畢 The first two characters are the same as in *Bremer*, but this name cannot be identified. Possibly it may refer to Lieutenant HADFIELD, who, however, was not killed.

[c] 三山村

them, and captured two guns and 1,000 small-arms. ELLIOT hastened to the rescue, and, as the crowds of villagers became more numerous, had to seek the assistance of the prefect. At this moment only a quarter of the ransom money had been paid, and the Fu Kien marines just arrived that very day. If orders had been given to surround and slay the foreign soldiers and take the [civilian] foreigners prisoners, we might have held them as hostages, ordered the ships beyond the Bogue, and then discussed terms at leisure, entirely as it should have suited us. This is the seventh turning-point in Canton affairs. However, our generals had not the wit to see this, but sent the prefect to use his persuasive powers with the people. After a whole day, he at last succeeded in getting ELLIOT safely out of the crowd on board his ship. The foreign ships now left one after the other; some of the largest got ashore, and the country people offered to burn and plunder them; but K'IKUNG would not hear of it. Notwithstanding, a military graduate[a] did succeed in blowing up one of the foreign ships at Ch'ün-pi[b] [Chuenpee] by means of some fire-ships he had got together, and all the others then made off. Another success was that of the Fatshan volunteers, who got to the windward of the Kwai-kong[c] Fort, and killed a score or more of the enemy by throwing a

[a] 庚體群　　[b] 穿鼻　　[c] 龜岡

poisonous dust into their eyes. They also succeeded in routing a foreign sampan sent to the rescue. All these facts were duly reported to the Emperor, who sarcastically replied, that the "village volunteers had "apparently been able to accomplish more than the "whole of the armies of China!" ELLIOT, too, was very much mortified, and issued a "proclamation," forsooth, calling upon the people "not to test the "leniency of Great England's officers again!" The people sent him a defiant reply saying:—"As you pro- "fess that your ships and guns are invincible, why did "you not attack Canton during Commissioner LIN's "viceroyalty? The other day, when you were "surrounded, why could not you fight your way out "without begging aid from the prefect? Having now " entrapped our disloyal statesmen into peace proposals " and withdrawal of the troops, you succeeded in " getting far into the country. If you dare to show "your faces in the river again, and we do not " assemble in myriads to burn your ships and " annihilate your ugly selves, then we are not good " subjects of the Great Ts'ing Empire!" At this juncture there were 36,000 volunteers training night and day in the two Canton districts; and, when ELLIOT heard of these preparations, he dared not accept the challenge, but, knowing that it was hopeless to regain trade at Canton, changed his policy; and a month later the Amoy affair occurred.

WEI YÜAN the historian, in summing up, remarks that it was the closing of trade, and not the forced surrender of the opium, that brought on the Canton War, the events leading to which were, the objections, generally, to sign away the lives of opium traders, and, specifically to deliver over the homicide. [Great Britain had already sacrificed the gunner of the "Lady Hughes" in 1784, and the Americans the Italian TERRANUOVA in 1821]. It is plain that ELLIOT had not a rebellious heart, inasmuch as he offered to agree to confiscation, offered rewards for the discovery of the murderer, and wished to await news from home. Finally, the laws provide for the ransom of Mongols and other uncivilized criminals by a fine in cattle, so that our demands upon him were altogether too exacting. The Rear-Admiral HAN should have been executed for his corruption, instead of being merely degraded. The Hoppo and his men, whose irregular charges more than doubled the regular import duties, and who had been battening for years upon the co-hong merchants, should have been compelled, instead of the latter, to pay for the war. It would have been better to sacrifice the Customs' interests for a time; to devote full attention to measures of defence, and, by abolishing the Hoppo's extortions, to secure the good-will of the other foreigners. Just as the Astronomical Board avails itself of foreign astronomers' labours, so we might have got a few Americans, Dutchmen, and Portuguese to instruct skilled Chinese artificers at Canton in the art of shipbuilding, and have offered to purchase foreign ships, guns, rockets, and powder from any persons wishing to sell. Not only could we have obtained these articles in exchange for our produce, but we might have accepted them in payment of duties. In this way we might have been content to extract a few millions only from the co-hong merchants, and in a short time we should have been able to confront foreign skill with Chinese skill. We could have leisurely strengthened the walls of outer Canton and the forts upon the river; got our armies properly together, and trained them up to naval tactics, gradually extending the same reforms to Amoy, Ningpo, and Shanghai; after which a grand review of all the fleets might have been held at Tientsin, and such a spectacle of naval greatness witnessed as China had never seen before. What enemy would then have dared to attack us? How could opium then have ventured into China? What slanderers would have then dared to open their mouths? This would have been what may be called "setting your own house in order first." Why, then, the hurry to make a show on the high seas and abroad? Some say that if the efforts of Commissioner LIN, who preserved the proud integrity of Canton without charging for a single extra soldier, had been imitated farther north, the Emperor would have had no cause for serious anxiety at all, and the island pirates would have been reduced to impotence; that, therefore, it is unfair to lay all the blame on him, instead of on the unpreparedness in the north, and the cowardice afterwards shewn at Canton. Moreover, LIN earnestly recommended that foreigner should be got to fight foreigner after the fall of Ting-hai, and that the integrity of our possessions should be maintained, and the three millions at Canton spent upon ships and guns. What a pity his advice was not tried !———WEI YÜAN agrees with the popular verdict that trade should not have been stopped,—but with the reservation that opium should not have been included any more in the trade, and that steps should have been taken to prevent the English from taking advantage of the weakness of China's maritime preparations to act as HIDEYOSHI[a] once acted in Corea and KOXINGA[b] in Formosa. WEI YÜAN here reads a lecture upon the subject of not interfering with the man at the wheel, or with the driver of the coach who is entrusted with the reins: but this literary effort of his in no way concerns the story, and is omitted from this translation.

[a] 平秀吉   [b] 鄭成功

PART II.

THE NANKING TREATY.

PART II.

THE NANKING TREATY.

THE yielding to terms on the part of the English at Canton in May 1841 was owing partly to our armies having to escape from immediate peril, and partly to the anxiety of the enemy to replenish his military chest with our money; so that neither side had leisure to think of trade arrangements: and the foreign soldiers, knowing, after their narrow escape at Sám-yün Village, that they had drawn upon themselves the hatred of the people of Canton, whose ferocity they now had reason to fear, did not dare to enter the Canton River any more for purposes of trade. The co-hong merchants were unwilling to go to Hongkong on account of the perils of the sea, and therefore it was proposed to exchange Hongkong for Tsím-sha Point and Cowloon. As the Emperor had not yet been invited to agree to Hongkong being given up, the Tartar-General and the Viceroy felt that the other two places were still more out of the question, and therefore arranged that [the foreigners] should come to Whampoa as before. But the enemy would not allow us to repair the Bogue Forts, which they razed, conveying the masonry to Hongkong for use there. They also wanted us to remove the piles and other obstructions in the river. Whilst haggling was going on as to these points, trade existed only in name. The prefect had agreed with ELLIOT to pay a military indemnity of six million dollars in addition to the value of the opium; but the Tartar-General called the former sum a "balance owing by the co-hong merchants," and never reported the latter at all. As soon as the foreign ships had withdrawn, we re-blocked the more important river-approaches, and rebuilt the forts; and, in short, put our defences in such a state that the enemy could not force his way in as before. The hostile community now blamed ELLIOT for not having exacted another port, and spread a report that the King of England had blamed him for incapacity, and had appointed as military general in his stead POTTINGER,[a] who was going up the coast, and would repeat the demands made last year at Tientsin. [He arrived on the 10th of August.]

There was a typhoon at Hongkong in July [21st], and K'IKUNG joined ILIANG in despatching a hasty memorial, which reported that innumerable foreign ships had been dashed to pieces, innumerable foreign soldiers and Chinese traitors swept into the sea; that all their tents and mat-sheds, the

[a] 璞鼎查

new Praya, etc., had been utterly annihilated; that the sea was literally covered with corpses; and so on. The Emperor thereupon returned solemn thanks to the god of the seas, and announced the event to the whole Empire. Over a hundred promotions were sanctioned for the gallant defence of Canton;—and meanwhile the whole fleet of foreign ships had gone to Fu Kien and taken Amoy! When Amoy was attacked the previous year, the Admiral CH'ÊN[a] had lost no time in obtaining sick-leave. TÊNG T'ING-CHÊNG and the *taotai* LIU YAO-CH'UN[b] had confined themselves to defending the old forts and piling up ramparts of sand, the natural strength of which kept the enemy off. Admiral YEN PÊH-T'AO,[c] on taking over charge, at once denounced his predecessor's cowardice in the most furious terms, and likewise K'ISHEN and YANG FANG for recommending peace at Canton: but he was in fact himself only a bragging and self-glorifying fool. He represented TÊNG's cautious, defensive policy in slighting terms, and requested the Emperor's sanction to an expenditure of two million taels, to be spent on fifty new ships of war, with which he proposed to sweep the English from the seas. He raised 9,000 new infantry and marines, and built three new forts on the islands off Amoy, all of which preparation proved waste labour when the news arrived of the peace

[a] 陳堦平 [b] 劉耀春 [c] 顏伯壽

negotiations at Canton, and the new levies had to be dismissed. On the 26th of August, however, the foreign fleets appeared suddenly off Amoy, and handed in a document calling for the surrender of the port until all the demands made the previous year at Tientsin should have been conceded. The next morning the ships sailed into the inner harbour, and began to reconnoitre with steam-launches in order to find out the range and direction of our guns, which were ascertained to be all fixtures; after which, of course, they kept out of range. A number of boats now advanced together, and their attack was met by our soldiers stationed on Kulang Sü and on two of the other islands. Two steam-launches and one man-of-war were sunk, and one mast was damaged besides. Two or three of their ships now concentrated their fire on one fort, and, after this had fallen, proceeded to another, causing considerable loss of life. Finally the great fort was attacked, and our dismissed marines turned renegade and assisted in the attack. YEN and LIU beat a retreat at the same moment; the pirates landed, and turned our own guns upon the city of Amoy, the public buildings, markets, etc., of which place were demolished within twenty-four hours; YEN and LIU retired upon T'ung-an[a] city, and Amoy fell into the pirates' hands, [with a loss of two killed and seven wounded]. However, the foreigners,

[a] 同安

having thus possessed themselves of Amoy, did not keep it, but proceeded in a few days with the greater part of their fleet on to Ningpo, leaving only a few ships anchored off Kulang Sü. Accordingly, about the 22nd of September, Admiral YEN reported the "recapture" of Amoy to the Emperor; but the sub-prefect of the place remained in hiding notwithstanding, and did not venture to re-assume his official duties. The Emperor degraded the Admiral to the third rank, but left him at his post, and despatched the under-secretary TWANHWA[a] to ascertain the true facts for his information. Meanwhile the foreigners on Kulang Sü were employing workmen to build for them more boats, with a view to reconnoitring up the river. With thirty of these, and five larger vessels, they advanced up the Muh-chwang Creek,[b] and sank five of our war-junks with their guns. Two of our captains were killed, but a resistance was offered by the Admiral and Rear-Admiral in charge, who succeeded in sinking one large foreign vessel. The enemy then withdrew out into the open sea. They dared not venture up the Five Tiger Passage of the Foochow River, for this only contains enough water when the tide is in.

To return to Ningpo. The foreign fleet had already left Ting-hai when YÜK'IEN arrived in January as Imperial Commissioner in succession to

[a] 端華   [b] 木樁港

ILIPU, and the Generals in command did their best to repair the walls and fortifications, and to get their troops together again. YÜK'IEN was as hot-headed as YEN PEH-T'AO, and totally ignorant of warfare: he was entirely in the hands of LIN TSÊH-SÜ—so long as LIN TSÊH-SÜ was there: but, owing to the Canton Salt Commissioner having, at an audience of the Emperor, vigorously supported K'ISHEN at the expense of LIN, LIN was ordered, first to Kashgaria, and then to the Yellow River works, so that the affairs of Chê Kiang were left more without a guiding head than ever. At best Ting-hai was but a solitary island, not worth defending at the cost of weakening the mainland armies. To make matters worse, all the three Brigadiers were destitute of military science or strategy, and would have built one great wall enclosing as an hypothenuse the outer as well as the inner town, which was hemmed in on the other sides by the mountains, had the absurdity of such a system of defence not been dinned into YÜK'IEN's ears by the people. The result was that nothing was done at all, let alone anything sensible. . When the news of the peace and orders to disband came, five thousand of the best soldiers were at Ting-hai, four thousand more being stationed at different points around Chên-hai and Ningpo. About the beginning [the 4th] of September the foreign ships [the

"Nemesis"] first attacked Shíh P'u,[a] but were unable to do much damage on account of the rocks: they then cruised up and down for a time, and finally attacked Ting-hai on the 26th of September. Our guns damaged one of the steam-launches, which made off at once. Two days later, the whole fleet commenced an attack upon the Hiao-fêng Hill,[b] but our troops were protected by the rocks, and a party of men who landed in a boat were driven off by our gingalls. Attacks made in other parts of the island were also repulsed by our guns. On the 1st of October, the pirates took advantage of the exhausted state of our troops to advance from three different points, so as to confuse us; and the boats of one party were sent back, so as to prevent the men from thinking of retreat. As the front ranks of the pirates fell, they were filled up from the rear. Our guns on the heights could not do much against a contrary wind, and by midday got too overheated to use. The pirates then recklessly scaled the hills and entered the city, the three Brigadiers all losing their lives in the fight: and thus Ting-hai fell a second time. [The *Repository* says that the Chinese defence was very noble.]

With regard to the 4,000 troops garrisoning Chên-hai, YÜK'IEN employed about 1,000 of them to guard

[a] 石浦 the scene of the French attack in 1885.
[b] 曉峯嶺

the precincts of the city; the General YÜ PU-YÜN[a] occupied Chao-pao Shan[b] with another 1,000; and the Brigadier SIE CH'AO-ÊN[c] defended Golden Fowl Hill across the river with a third. Observing a white flag hoisted on Chao-pao Shan, YÜK'IEN saw that YÜ PU-YÜN was unfaithful, and did his best to rouse the religious patriotism of the soldiers; whilst YÜ PU-YÜN pretended that his foot so ailed him that he could not kneel down to join in the solemn vow. YÜK'IEN reported to the Emperor that the foreign ships had, including black soldiers and disloyal Chinese, a force of quite 10,000 men; and that his idea was to defend the several critical points if the pirate fleet advanced in one body, and to work at the defences day and night should they defer the attack. He pointed out the disadvantages under which the Chinese lay in point of discipline and unity as compared with the invaders; but vowed not to leave Chên-hai alive, or to receive any propositions from the enemy on that account. On the 10th of October the foreign fleet attacked the above-mentioned three positions. General YÜ and his men bolted without firing a shot, and the force on Golden Fowl Hill was soon silenced and routed. Seeing that there was no escape for Chên-hai, YÜK'IEN sent his aide-de-camp to the Governor with the Imperial Commissioner's seal, and

[a] 余步雲 [b] 招寶山 [c] 謝朝恩

drowned himself in a pond.[a] On the 13th, four men-of-war, two steam-launches, and a flotilla of boats appeared before Ningpo, whence Yü Pu-yün again bolted, followed by the *taotai* and the prefect[b] Têng T'ing-ts'ai, to Shang-yü city. The cities of Ts'z-k'i and Yü-yao were captured by small boats, were found deserted by their populations, and were plundered and burnt: robber bands started up; and the whole province was thrown into a state of panic. The dastardly Yü Pu-yün reported to the Emperor that poor Yük'ien had been the first to flee; and spread a report that the foreigners had attacked Ningpo in order to avenge the death of the white barbarian Wên-li,[c] whose head had been stuck upon a pole during the summer by Yük'ien. This was represented to the Emperor by the Governor Liu Yün-k'o;[d] but, unfortunately for this argument, the enemy had already gone back on his treaty at Canton, unsuccessfully demanded Cowloon and Tsim-sha, and refused permission to rebuild the Bogue Forts; and had moreover already announced his intention to take Amoy first and Ting-hai

[a] He was rescued, but swallowed gold afterwards, and expired near Yü-yao city.—*Repository*.

[b] 鄭廷彩 brother of the Viceroy Têng.

[c] 嗢哩 Captain Stead. of the "Pestonjee Bomanjee," was murdered by Yük'ien or his minions.—*Repository*.

[d] 劉韻珂

afterwards: finally, the foreigners had stated by proclamation and letter that their intention was to exact ports for trade, not saying one word about Yük'ien. And it may here be mentioned in anticipation that, the following year, when Ilipu at Cha-p'u asked the British chief why he was again invading us, the letter of reply contained not one word alluding to Yük'ien, whose only fault was that his capacity was not equal to his ardour. [The British losses at Ting-hai and Chên-hai were 17 killed and 36 wounded.]

The Emperor now appointed the imperial clansman Yikking[a] as Generalissimo, with two other Manchu dignitaries as advisers. Niu Kien,[b] Governor of Ho Nan, was appointed Viceroy at Nanking, and Iliang was made Imperial Commissioner for Fu Kien. Niu's idea was to hire as many braves, robbers, and scoundrels of all descriptions as could be got together from the provinces; to keep up a harassing guerilla warfare; and to station agents in the places occupied by the foreigners, so as to prepare for rendering assistance when a suitable time should come. The Ningpo people, like the Cantonese, were put down as "disloyal." All this was approved by the Emperor, who ordered Yikking to put the enemy off guard by discharging his functions in the first instance from Soochow. There his staff behaved so

[a] 奕經   [b] 牛鑑

extravagantly and dissolutely that he decided to remove his head-quarters to Kia-hing [Kashing]. Here he and one of his advisers both had an identical dream, to the effect that the foreigners had swarmed on board their ships, and had left in a panic; which fitted in exactly with a piece of intelligence, reported from Ningpo that very day, to the effect that the foreigners were getting their arms on board the ships. This filled them both with a desire to fight at once; and the whole party, suites included, proceeded to Hangchow, where the second adviser, T‘ÊHISHUN,[a] was placed in charge, whilst YIKKING, with his fellow dreamer WÊNWEI,[b] went to Shao-hing city.

Now there had been a great deal of snow during the winter, followed by heavy rains, so that all the stock of fire-boats and the fuel collected was out of condition and useless. Notwithstanding the prayers of everyone that he would postpone the attack for at least a fortnight, YIKKING obstinately refused to wait, and fixed the 15th of March, 1842, as the date for the recovery of the occupied cities in full force, thus ignoring the previously agreed upon arrangement about guerilla fighting. The enemy, hearing of these preparations, naturally prepared themselves too: the foreign officers all went on board, leaving only a few hundred men in charge of the large guns on the city wall, to deal with any army advan-

[a] 特依順   [b] 文蔚

cing by the west gate. At Chên-hai they proceeded to take possession of the Chao-pao Shan, so as to be able to bombard thence our men as they poured into that city. This was the *interpretation* of the dream! Our troops were strictly enjoined not to use fire or rockets, lest they should set fire to the town; the only thing to be done was to try and get the Chinese traitors to betray the foreigners, especially the chiefs, into our hands, when the recapture of the cities would be easy, and we could arrange our own terms with the hostages in our hands. YIKKING entrenched himself with 3,000 men in the east suburb of Shao-hing. WÊNWEI occupied the heights of CH‘ANG-K‘I,[a] one mile from Ts‘z-k‘i city, with 4,000 men, half of whom were under Colonel CHU,[b] and intended for an attack on Chên-hai. General TWAN YUNG-FUH[c] lay concealed outside the walls of Ningpo with 4,000 men, destined for an attack upon that city; and a Colonel with 1,000 more men guarded the Ningpo and Chên-hai road at Camel Bridge, half way between the two cities. Boats were also sunk at Mei Hü;[d] so as to prevent river communication; and a reserve force of volunteers was stationed at Shang-yü city. When the appointed time came, our men marched towards the west gate, when, the guard having been killed by our friends in the city, who also spiked the guns on

[a] 長溪嶺   [b] 朱桂   [c] 叚永福   [d] 梅墟

the walls, the men advanced through the gate right up to the prefect's and magistrate's *yaméns* before the foreigners knew what was taking place. Then followed a street fight, and our troops found themselves taken in the rear by a foreign force which had come to the rescue from the north gate. Finding it impossible to withstand the rockets and guns with which the foreigners peppered them from the housetops, they retired, fighting as they went, with a loss of 250 men. General TWAN, coming up with reinforcements, turned round and bolted, not even attempting to rally the men, or even to fall back upon and defend his camp at Ta-yin Shan.[a] General YÜ PU-YÜN, who was advancing with 2,000 men from Fung-hwa, as soon as he heard of the defeat, turned and fled all night long into the open country. So much for our arms at Ningpo. Of the force at Ts'z-k'i, a part, that is 500 men, succeeded in getting into Chên-hai in the same way as had been done at Ningpo; but our agents in the city were too few to secure the persons of the pirates, and it was daylight before our fire-arms could be sent for. The enemy then gave us a broadside from his position on Chao-pao Shan, which drove our men helter-skelter out of the city. Colonel CHU, with his reinforcements, lost his way in the wind and rain, and never came up to Chên-hai at all. So much for

[a] 大隱山

our arms at Chên-hai. Then it was that the error of all these hasty arrangements was manifest: but no irreparable disaster had yet occurred, as our total losses did not exceed 300 men. The position at Ts'z-k'i was again re-occupied with 1,700 men, and the city itself was guarded by volunteers. YIKKING neglected alike to decapitate the cowardly generals, and to himself advance up to Shang-yü; and, as the commander of the local volunteers at Ts'z-k'i was sent for to consult on the situation, the volunteers found themselves left without a head, and so dispersed. A week later, the enemy sent steam-launches to burn our fire-boats, and landed between 2,000 and 3,000 men to attack our position near Ts'z-k'i: as before, their boats were withdrawn to prevent the men from thinking of retreat. Colonel CHU met them with 400 of his men armed with gingalls. Over 400 foreign soldiers were killed, including their chief PA-MEH-TSUN [a] [? Bramston], not one of our men being even wounded behind their shelter. If at this moment the foreigners could only have been taken in the rear, we might have gained a complete victory; or even if we had had a few hundred men to guard the rear of our position on the hill, we might at least have prevented a defeat. WÊNWEI's camp was only a few miles off; but he refused to send any re-inforce-

[a] 巴麥尊

ments until the evening, when it was too late; for the foreigners had then taken us in the rear, and defeated us, Colonel CHU and his son both falling in the fight. The enemy was exceedingly unlikely to have gone on to Ch'ang-k'i that night: but the cowardly WÊNWEI deserted his position and bolted during the darkness, distributing lavish rewards to boatmen and chairmen as he went, so as to escape the pursuit of the English. As he had bolted, his troops naturally broke too, leaving all their stores and arms to take care of themselves. WÊNWEI then reported to the Emperor that his camp had been burnt by "disloyal Chinese;" whereas the English had not come up even on the evening of the following day! The idea which now suggested itself was to fix the head-quarters at Shang-yü, entice the foreign soldiers farther inland, and to try fight after fight in order to prevent their harrying Kiang Su province, and in order to discourage them from placing their demands too high. YIKKING and WÊNWEI, however, had now completely lost their heads. They represented to the Emperor that only seven of our men had escaped alive in one fight, in which, as a matter of fact, only seven had been even wounded; that over a thousand instead of just over a hundred had been killed at Ts'i-k'i; and that 17,000 English instead of between 2,000 and 3,000 had landed there. They then retired from

Shao-hing to Si-hing, whence YIKKING finally crossed to Hangchow. These were our efforts by land.

Our naval programme had been to collect a force of fishing boats at Cha-p'u, and endeavour to recapture Ting-hai : over 10,000 marines had been stationed in various places with this object in view; but YIKKING continued to listen to the craven counsels of his aide-de-camp JUNGCHAO,[a] and ordered them to disperse : he also withdrew the war-junks and fire-boats, in consequence of which the destitute fisherman marines now went over to the foreigners. These were our doings afloat. There was one officer, CHÊNG TING-CH'ÊN,[b] notwithstanding, who had the courage to disobey orders, and YIKKING was half inclined to listen to JUNGCHAO's advice to have him executed, only refraining from this dastardly act owing to the indignant remonstrances of TSANG HÜ-CH'ING,[c] the *literatus* who had originally recommended guerilla warfare. YIKKING now ventured back across the river once more, and issued orders in all directions for all the soldiers to fight as they best could : the result of this was that over 300 British and Sikh heads were brought in within a fortnight : also four English officers and over 50 soldiers, white and black, were sent prisoners to Ningpo, with two disloyal Chinese advisers. Meanwhile CHÊNG TING-CH'ÊN, with his fire-boats, managed to

[a] 容照　　[b] 鄭鼎臣　　[c] 臧紆青

burn or sink four large men-of-war and about a dozen boats, during which operations from 500 to 600 foreign sailors were drowned. The magistrate of Chên-hai also earned a laurel by a bold attack upon the fleet in the open, off Chên-hai, and YIKKING received a double peacock's feather in consequence; whilst the two heroes themselves received proportionate rewards. This created a tremendous commotion at head-quarters. Those who had defended CHÊNG clamoured for their share of notice, whilst those who had attacked him vowed that the victory was imaginary.[a] The Governor LIU YÜN-K'O[b] became the mouthpiece of the second clique; but CHÊNG closed their mouths by sending four large boats full of charred and splintered foreign planks, as well as the heads and original clothes of his pirate victims. The Governor, however, had already asked that ILIPU might come to Ningpo to discuss terms of peace, and the Emperor had appointed the imperial clansman K'IYING[c] as Imperial Commissioner, to be assisted by the Acting Tartar-General at Hangchow and by one TS'ISHÊN[d] as associates. They were ordered not to advance, nor to take the heads of stray barbarians, the penalty for doing which was now declared capital. The

[a] The *Repository* of 1842, pages 455 and 470, shews that this victory was purely imaginary. No fight took place at all, still less was any foreigner killed.

[b] 劉韻珂　　[c] 耆英　　[d] 齊愼

repairs to the Yellow River having now been completed, LIN TSÊH-SÜ was again ordered to Kashgaria, and the Grand Secretary WANG TING,[a] who had been associated with him, died of grief and mortification. Meanwhile the English made reconnoitring expeditions round Shanghai and up the Yangtsze; obtained at Ningpo maps of the Empire and charts of the Yangtsze and Yellow River; turned our discharged fisherman marines into pilots and guides; manufactured a number of small boats for use in the creeks; and exacted from the gentry of Ningpo, as the price of their retirement, an indemnity of $200,000, withdrawing on board their ships on the 7th of May. YIKKING and his party accordingly reported that he had "forced the British troops to retire," and had recovered Ningpo. The real facts were that a steamer had been sent to England to report the capture of Ningpo, and that six months later a reply had been received from the King ordering the ships to proceed again to Tientsin to ask for open ports and free trade, the retirement of the troops from Ningpo having nothing whatever to do with the movements of our armies. Towards the middle of May the foreign ships at Chên-hai also left the place for the north, leaving only four ships and 1,000 men in charge of Ting-hai. The two promontories[b] at the mouth of the Hangchow River

[a] 王鼎　　　[b] 龜山, 蛇山

had lately silted up so much[a] that the foreigners could not get up to Hangchow with ships; but on the 18th of May they bombarded Cha-p'u, and landed a force to attack the east gate. Here they were met by troops from Shen Si and Kan Suh armed with gingalls, receiving such rough treatment that they went round to the south gate. As the Manchu garrison had been in the habit of calling the Chinese "disloyalists," the Fu Kien braves sided with the enemy and set fire to the town. The foreigners then got over the wall and burnt the Manchu quarter,[b] the Assistant Tartar-General and the Acting Sub-Prefect losing their lives, and the *taotai* escaping to Kashing, which place, as also Hangchow, was now threatened too. When ILIPU arrived at Cha-p'u, the English demands were so extravagant that nothing definite could be arrived at; and, when the Governor requested the Emperor's sanction to the restoration of the score or two of white and black barbarian prisoners, the foreign ships had left Cha-p'u. The prisoners were then sent to Chên-hai, and it was suggested that bygones should be bygones; but the English would not listen any more. The Emperor ordered the Tartar-General or one of the Associates to proceed to Kashing; and on this YIK-

[a] See description of the southern sandbanks in the *Repository* for 1842, page 290.

[b] Ever since this the Assistant Tartar-General has had his office at Hangchow.

KING crossed over north. No sooner had the Imperial Commissioner K'IYING arrived at Kashing, than he received the Emperor's orders to go to Canton, and T'ÊHISHUN[a] was ordered to act as Tartar-General of Hangchow. This was because the Censor SU T'ING-K'WEI,[b] had represented that the Nepaulese had attacked the English garrisons in India, and that the fleet had to go to the rescue: accordingly K'IYING was ordered to see if he could not seize the opportunity to retake Hongkong. When matters became pressing at Nanking, he was equally suddenly ordered back, before he had reached Canton. At this time there were fourteen foreign ships at Hongkong; a score or two of sampans and small craft; about one thousand foreign soldiers; and a large sprinkling of disloyal Chinese. YIKSHAN having succeeded in drawing off over 3,000 of these last, the chief men of those remaining in Hongkong also for the most part shewed a wish to come back to their allegiance. These disloyalists proposed to put the Bogue Forts in order, take advantage of the winter neap tides, join with the Hongkong disloyalists, make a surprise attack on the fleet, and annihilate the whole foreign community at one blow: but YIKSHAN was afraid of exciting K'IKUNG's anger, and would not allow it. The Emperor deprived YIKSHAN of his chief official titles for his incapacity, and ILIANG

[a] 特依順　　[b] 蘇廷魁

was ordered to replace YEN PEH-T'AO, also degraded for failing to destroy the fleet at Amoy. On the 18th of the 4th moon the foreign ships left Cha-p'u,[a] and a number of them arrived off Wusung on the 3rd of the 5th moon; and on the 5th NIU KIEN received instructions from YIKKING to temporize: but, as he delayed sending his orders to the foreign fleet for two days, it was already too late. The Magistrate of Pao-shan city, near Wusung, had proposed to lay an ambush and entice the foreigners ashore, leaving the forts to themselves; but the infatuated NIU KIEN did nothing but allow the remnants of the troops, who had fled so ignominiously at Ningpo, to plunder the natives, who thus felt their hearts fill with rancour.

On the 16th of June, the General commanding at the forts opened fire upon the foreign ships, sinking two, cutting in two the masts of two others, and causing the death by drowning of over 200[b] foreign soldiers. The foreigners attacked Siao Sha-pei[c] in boats, routed with a ridiculously small force the cowardly contingent from Ningpo, landed a few men, killed the general with a cannon shot, and put to flight the several thousand soldiers who lined the bank.

[a] The forces withdrew from Chap'u on the 23rd May: the dates here appear to be somewhat confused, and cannot be identified.

[b] No such losses are mentioned in the *Repository*.

[c] 小沙背

Niu Kien fled to Kia-ting city, and the easternmost fort was also abandoned; so that Pao-shan city, with a vast amount of war *materiel*, fell into the enemy's hands; to the great consternation of Shanghai, which place was at once abandoned by both the civil and military authorities, who fled to Sung-kiang. The Fu Kien marines thereupon became bandits, and took to burning and plundering. On the 19th eight or nine foreign ships came up to Shanghai, but that city was already deserted. Two days later, the foreigners[a] took two steam-launches and four or five sampans up to a point near Sung-kiang, where they were opposed by 2,000 Shen Si and Kan Suh soldiers, and retired after a protracted fusillade on both sides, repeating the operation with the same results the next day; so that Sung-kiang escaped. The pirates next made a reconnaissance towards Soochow; but their launches were piloted by our fishermen on to the shallows, and had to go back. On the 23rd the ships withdrew to Wusung, intending to enter the Yangtsze. On the 18th of July they were off Kwa Chou; but, finding that city deserted, they turned to Chinkiang on the opposite side. Hailing, the Assistant Tartar-General[b] over the Manchu garrison there, was an imbecile creature,

[a] Admiral Parker with two small iron steamers proceeded about 50 miles above Shanghai on the 22nd June.—*Repository*, page 676.

[b] 海齡

and NIU KIEN, after failing to close the Wusung river to attack, should have hastened to Chinkiang, concerted measures of defence with the Associate TS'ISHÊN and the General LIU YÜN-HIAO,[a] and assumed supreme command over the Tartar HAILING: if this had been done, the foreign ships would not have gone straight on to Nanking, and we might have tried to burn them; or, anyhow, should have treated with them without being at their mercy. But NIU KIEN fled straight to Nanking, and HAILING told TS'ISHÊN and LIU to leave him alone and defend the outer city. He would not allow any one to leave the city, and slaughtered a number of disloyal Chinese, thereby exciting a general panic of indignation. He made no preparations, collected no stores for defence, and made no attempt to organize a volunteer force. The thousand or so of Manchu garrison troops, and the 600 Chinese troops were scattered about anyhow. The troops outside the city kept off those pirates who had landed during a couple of days; after which the English,[b] whilst making a feint of an attack upon the north gate, secretly sent a body of men to scale the wall on the south-west side, and swarmed into the city, with a loss of only one[c] or two men. The English first burnt the Manchu camp, HAILING

[a] 劉允孝　　　　[b] 21st July.
[c] The *Repository* says we lost 169 killed and wounded.

falling at the hands of his own men,[a] and Chinkiang was then given over to plunder and massacre. The Ningpo barbarian chieftain POTTINGER wished to proceed thence to Tientsin at once; but MORRISON prevented him, saying:—"This is the key to China's "rice-tribute supply, and as long as we keep our "finger on it, we shall have our own way;" and so he did not go. At this moment there were over eighty foreign ships thundering in the river, and reaching up as far as I-chêng,[b] where all the salt-junks were set on fire, notwithstanding the offer of Tls. 500,000 on the part of the Yang-chow salt-merchants. On the 9th of August the ships had all reached Nanking, and the Emperor, anxious about the tribute-rice communications, gave K'I-YING[c] carte blanche to act as he should see fit. The enemy had already received the King's instructions not to insist upon a military indemnity or the value of the opium, if only trading privileges were extended to the other provinces; and no more opium would come to China. It was for this reason that the foreign army left Ningpo in May, and issued a "proclamation" at Cha-p'u, saying that they were going to Tientsin to seek peace in accordance with the King's commands. ILIPU now sent CHANG HI[d] and

[a] The *Repository* says he committed suicide, and received high posthumous honours.

[b] 儀徵   [c] 耆英   [d] 張喜

others to the foreign ships. The foreign chieftains demanded [1] twenty million dollars, to be paid up over a period of three years; [2] Hongkong as a trading place; [3] permission to trade at Canton, Foochow, Amoy, Ningpo, and Shanghai; [4] foreign officials to be on terms of equality with Chinese officials; and the rest as proposed last year. CHANG HI said that $6,000,000 had already been given at Canton last year towards the indemnity and the opium, and asked if the money demand now made was not excessive, and the number of ports named too great altogether. MORRISON said:—" This is the sum we " require, and, of course, not the sum which China " offers. Moreover, our leading idea now is open " trade, and not to get money. If we only obtain " one or two ports for trade, China may decide for " herself about the indemnity and the opium :" but the high authorities, instead of giving a prompt answer, sent back CHANG HI with a message; and, whilst he was moving to and fro' during a period of two days, the enemy had learnt from disloyal Chinese that new troops were being ordered up, and said " that we were only trying to gain time, and that " unless an agreement were come to that day hostilities " would commence on the morrow;"—their desire being for a speedy peace, as they did not really expect to get all they asked. But all our leaders now lost courage, and sent a reply that night, submitting to everything, and not alluding at all to the rule about opium being excluded from China. The English were overjoyed, and our leaders followed the example of those at Canton after the Square Fort had fallen, and reported to the Emperor that the enemy's guns were on Mount Chung,[a] and that the whole of Nanking was at their mercy. They also pleaded that in times gone by "the Emperor K'IEN-LUNG, when un-"successful in Burmah, had abandoned 5,000 li of "territory beyond the frontier," thus maligning the acts of past sacred monarchs by trumping up false parallels; for, as a matter of fact, the slab over the T'ung-pih[b] Gate of Yün Nan declaring that "China's territory ends here" was put up by K'ANG-HI, whose maps, still extant, could hardly accuse his *successor* of having "lost" 5,000 li beyond it! The enemy also said that the document treating of conditions must bear the seal of the Emperor[c] of China, and that they would send it home by steamer to have the King's seal affixed, and that the ships would only retire to the sea-board; but that their troops at Chusan, Amoy, and Hongkong must remain three years, until the whole of the indemnities should have been paid up, when they would be withdrawn. The treaty was concluded on the 29th of August by K'IYING, ILIPU, and NIU

[a] 鍾山   [b] 銅壁關

[c] See Rescript of 8th September 1842.—*Repository*, page 629.

Kien, who went in person on board the enemy Pottinger's ship [the "Cornwallis"]. Two days later Pottinger, Morrison, etc., went into the city; and had an interview with our officials at the Chêng-kioh[a] Temple.[b] For days in succession drafts were made on the provincial treasuries of Kiang-ning, Soochow, and An Hwei, and on the salt treasury of Yangchow, and several millions of taels were thus presented to the foreigners. In the middle of October, as the foreign ships were about to leave, a banquet was given by our leaders at the Temple, and a few days later all the ships withdrew to Ting-hai. The Emperor now ordered up the Viceroy Niu Kien to be punished for not having guarded the mouth of the Yangtsze, and K'iying was appointed in his place. Ilipu was ordered from Chê Kiang to Canton as High Commissioner for the drawing up of trade regulations. Yikshan, Yikking, Wênwei, and Yü Pu-yün were are all cast into the Board of Punishments; but the last-named only was executed,—during the following winter. Punishments according to their several deserts were also meted out to the various civil and military officials along the coast who had lost their towns, and the districts annexed to the captured places were exempted from the payment of land-tax.

[a] 正覺寺
[b] The white flag was shewn on the 11th, and there were several conferences both ashore and afloat previous to the 29th.—*Repository*.

This winter there occurred the demand for the Formosa prisoners. The year before and the next year happened the breaking of faith on the part of the Nepaulese, French, and Americans, and the burning of the factory at Canton by volunteers. The Formosa prisoner case arose out of two reconnoitring visits paid by foreign ships to Formosa in the autumn of 1841 and the spring[a] of 1842. One was wrecked during a storm at Tamsui, and the other was led upon the shallows by native fishing-craft at Ta-an.[b] In both cases the local volunteers surrounded and made prisoners of the crews; captured one large three-masted ship, two sampans, twenty-four white, and a hundred and sixty-five black barbarians, twenty guns, a number of small-arms, and a quantity of Government property taken by the said pirates at Ningpo and Chên-hai. The Brigadier TAHUNGA[c] and the *taotai* YAO YING[d] had sent several memorials to the Emperor on the subject,[e] and in the spring of 1842 nineteen of the enemy's ships went to Formosa to take revenge. They were piloted in by native pirates; but, our troops having destroyed the pirate junks, the enemy fired a few

[a] March 10th.—*Repository*, 1842.
[b] 大安   [c] 達洪阿   [d] 姚瑩
[e] These were the cases of the ship "Nerbudda" and the brig "Ann," the defenceless crews of which were kept in miserable captivity, and finally massacred in cold blood by the order of the authorities. Sir HENRY POTTINGER'S correspondence upon the subject is contained in the *Repository* for 1843.

shots from a distance and decamped. The spies which they sent into T'aiwan from time to time were all taken and decapitated; so that Formosa was preserved entire. The Brigadier and the *taotai* received distinguished rewards at the Emperor's hands; but, after the Nanking peace, prisoners on both sides were to be restored, and it was found that the Emperor had, during the summer, ordered the decapitation of the 165 black barbarians; so that the white ones only were restored.[a] The enemy's eye, POTTINGER, then accused the Brigadier and the *taotai* of having wantonly massacred distressed British subjects. The peace party at Nanking were jealous of the success gained in Formosa, whilst the defeated authorities at Amoy felt particularly small. Rumours thus flew about; and K'IYING, acting upon private letters received from the Viceroy[b] and the General at Foochow, accused the Brigadier and *taotai* of obtaining unfair credit. The new Viceroy was ordered to proceed to Formosa and report, when it appeared that the Brigadier and the *taotai* had simply quoted the statements sent in by their subordinates. As it was impossible to convict on this, pressure was put upon the Brigadier and *taotai* to force them to own up, in order to appease the for-

[a] Six whites and three natives of India were restored.—*Repository*, 1842, page 648.

[b] 蘇廷玉; evidently brother of the Censor.

eigners; and they were both summoned to Peking. The soldiers became mutinous on hearing this news; but the accused themselves prevailed on their troops to remain quiet. The Viceroy resigned, and his successor sent all the correspondence up to Peking; when the Emperor, seeing how unfair it was to blame the Brigadier and the *taotai*, did not punish them severely, and soon restored them to favour.

The Ghoorkas are south-west of Tibet, and conterminous with the British East Indian possession Bengal, with which district they had a standing feud. Hearing in 1839 of the British raid, they represented to the Resident in Tibet that " they were neighbours " of the P'ilêng*ᵃ* tribe belonging to Tili, and were " always being insulted by them; that, the Tili*ᵇ* " now being at war with a metropolitan possession, " they, the Ghoorkas, would be glad to attack the " Tili possessions in order to assist the Celestial " chastisement." If only our ministers had known anything about geography or foreign politics, and allowed them to create a diversion, then England's Indian troops would have had their hands full at home, and could not all have come to China. This was our first offer of assistance from abroad: but our ministers, not knowing that the Tili were the English, that P'ilêng was Bengal, and that the Metropolitan Possession was Canton in China, re-

ᵃ 披楞   *ᵇ* 底里 (? Delhi).

plied that "the Heavenly Dynasty never concerns "itself with the mutual tiltings of savages;" and thus the Ghoorka barbarians abandoned the idea of attacking India, and the soldiers with which England made her raids entertained no uneasiness about India at all. After the Nanking peace in the autumn of 1842, the British on their return to India ironically asked the Ghoorkhas to "come on:" the Ghoorkhas then turned upon the Residents, whom they addressed in very insubordinate terms. The Residents only just managed to keep them to a nominal allegiance.

France and America are both powerful countries of the west, and, like the English, trade at Canton. They are hereditary enemies of England, but very obsequious to China. The previous year, when the English attacked China, and stopped all trade by blockading the coast, the other countries were very indignant, and said that, if the English did not return home soon, they would also bring up men-of-war to Canton and call them to account,—as LIN TSÊH-SÜ twice represented to the Emperor. All of a sudden LIN TSÊH-SÜ was cashiered, and K'ISHEN thought of nothing but peace; so the matter fell short. In March,[a] when K'ISHEN was marched off a prisoner, the American head-man came a few days after to try and arrange matters. Hence came the suggestions that trade and no other demands should be

[a] 12th March 1841.—*Repository*.

granted, and that ships smuggling opium should be confiscated with their cargoes. But the leaders in Canton made a night attack upon the factories, and killed several Americans by mistake; so that the Americans were no longer willing to come forward in our interests.

After the repeated breaches of their convention by the English, the French foreign official several times offered his assistance in building ships. That winter two men-of-war arrived, with a military leader, who said he had some confidential business upon which he wished to confer with the Tartar-General: he begged that the services of an interpreter might be dispensed with, as he had two bonzes with him who understood Chinese. The Tartar-General YIKSHAN and the Viceroy K'IKUNG had several interviews with him outside the city. The attendants[a] were dismissed, and it was confidentially represented that, the English having stopped the trade of all nations, the French King had sent men-of-war for protection, and had ordered him to act as mediator, and to proceed to Ningpo and Shanghai to arrange peace, when he would have no difficulty in bringing the English to a proper sense of things, and in finding a way out of their

[a] The *Repository* for 1842 says that an interview was held on the 22nd March between YIKSHAN and Col. DE JANCIGNY; M. CHALLAYE, the French Consul, was present. The "bonzes" were evidently French or native Catholics, in Chinese dress.

greedy demands. If the English would not agree, he would find some pretext for fighting them. This was our second offer of assistance from abroad: but YIKSHAN at first refused even to represent the matter to the Emperor. The French then suggested that they should, as a first step, go to Hongkong and see POTTINGER. After several days' discussion, they replied that the English demanded Hongkong and three millions [? of taels] for the opium. YIKSHAN still declined to forward their representations to the Emperor. At last, when he did so, he added:—"but "the enemy's designs are unfathomable, and possibly "they are really assisting the English in an under- "hand way, and acting as spies on us for them." The French hung on from February to June, awaiting our commands; and at last in June proceeded to Wusung:[a] but the English were already far up the Yangtsze. The French wanted to engage Chinese pilots to take them up; but the Shanghai officials, on the contrary, threw obstacles in their way; and so much time was occupied in trying to obtain pilots that, at last, when the French entered the river in other boats, the treaty of peace was already concluded,[b] and the English had got all they wanted;— anyhow a vast deal more than the French had proposed on their behalf. The French head-man

[a] The "Erigone" arrived there on the 26th June.
[b] Captain CECILLE arrived in a junk just in time to witness the ceremony.—*Repository*, page 680.

went back much mortified; and the following winter returned to Canton to arrange about trade. The English desired that traders of all nations should report to them first, and then pay duties; but the French and the Americans indignantly exclaimed:— " We are no dependencies of England, nor have we " been treacherous and bullying. Why then treat " them better than us?" On this some American ships of war entered port, and, a few months later, some Frenchmen too. Both of them submitted letters, begging to pay tribute, and to be allowed to express their devotion at an interview. They also requested to be allowed to leave their ships in the south, whilst the tribute-envoys and a small suite went overland to Peking; for they wished to make some confidential suggestions, and to assist us,—as the Uigurs once assisted the T'ang dynasty against the rebel ANLUHSHAN. This was the third offer of assistance from abroad; rejected, however, repeatedly by our ministers. ILIPU had already died at Canton; and in 1843 K'IYING was ordered thither to carry on his work: permission had been granted[a] to one country after another to trade on the same terms as England without the interference of the co-hong merchants, and with liberty to go to the other ports, and stand on a footing of equality

[a] K'IYING'S proclamation is published in the *Repository* for 1843.

with the mandarinate; so that the English even became *patrons* of the others.

The history of the volunteers or patriots of Canton is as follows. When the English were hard pressed at San-yüan Village, in the summer of 1841, they hesitated about coming to trade at Canton any more. But, after the peace, Canton was declared open by imperial decree, and the following winter the white barbarians went insolently all about the place. The exasperated people rose upon them, burnt and plundered the factory,[a] and killed some foreign officers and soldiers off Macao. The ships of the chief POTTINGER were then at Canton, but dared not take any revenge. The Viceroy and Governor, however, punished the offenders in order to give satisfaction: but P'AN SHIH-CH'ÊNG,[b] a gentleman of Canton, engaged at his own expense a French foreign official named LEI-JÊN-SZ[c] [? Colonel DE JANCIGNY] to order some ships and guns from France, and also some torpedoes for attacking ships under the water. Four two-masted men-of-war, as strong and well-built as any foreign ship, were thus built at his expense, at a cost of

[a] 7th December 1842.—See *Repository* for 1842, page 687.

[b] 潘仕成

The *Repository* for 1833, page 350, says that P'AN KIQUA, father of the senior hong merchant, had been disgusted by seeing the tyranny practised in Manila.

[c] 雷任士

Tls. 20,000 for each ship, and Tls. 40 for each torpedo. On this the Emperor ordered the building of a new Canton fleet to be confided to him, quite free of all official interference, so as to prevent peculation; but, owing to the obstacles thrown in the way by the high authorities, the matter dropped.[a] Thus China was neither without allies or internal zeal in the pirate war: but she had no one to take the reins in hand; and so her dependent barbarians were driven over to aid her enemy, and her brave people were turned into disloyalists: her patriots were even denounced as obstinate persons.

Of late, with the trade all along the coast, the opium business is greater than ever; and, at the recommendation of the Canton Governor HWANG ÊN-T'UNG,[b] the prohibitions against Roman Catholicism have been relaxed throughout the Empire. The foreigners in possession of Ting-hai and Kulang Sü put pressure on the officials, and harbour all sorts of outlaws; whilst the man at Wu-shih Shan in Foochow [*i.e.* H.B.M. Consul] occupies the very heart of the capital, and can look over the whole city. The Governor-General and the Governor look helplessly on, and represent to the Emperor "that " they have only given him a tumble-down temple

[a] The *Repository* for 1843, page 108, mentions an American as having been employed by native gentry.

[b] 黃恩彤

"*outside* the city!" The gentry and people of Foochow are highly indignant; and Lin Tsêh-sü, who is with his family, is in the specially black books of the high authorities there.

In 1844, K'iying was recalled, and Hwang Ên-t'ung was degraded to the rank of sub-prefect and sent home. In 1845 the English called upon us to keep K'iying's promise to admit them into the city after three years, and to allow the establishment of an office there; but the Viceroy Sü Kwang-tsin,[a] with the co-operation of the patriots in the city and the Americans outside of it, succeeded in repelling them, and the enemy was constrained to retire *re infectâ*. The Viceroy was made a viscount for this, and the Governor Yeh Ming-shên[b] was made a baron. Things were now tolerably quiet at Canton. The new Emperor, Hien-fung, as soon as he came to the throne in 1851, issued a special decree doing justice to the memories of Lin Tsêh-sü, Yao Ying, and Tahunga for their efforts to maintain the integrity of the outlying parts of the Empire, and censuring K'iying's timidity and his error in defying the enemy. This decree was received with great satisfaction.[c]

The barbarian pirate war lasted two years in all, and cost Tls. 70,000,000. There was always a

[a] 徐廣縉 [b] 葉明琛, Commissioner Yeh, of 1860.
[c] These last paragraphs seem to have been added on to a subsequent edition.

clamour for either peace or war; but no one, strange to say, ever recommended a strictly defensive attitude. Again, fighting was neglected when fighting was proper, and indulged in when out of place: so, also, peace was neglected when peace was proper, and peace was decided for exactly at the wrong time. Such defensive measures as we took were taken at wrong places, and neglected where really required. Instead of putting herself on the defensive, Canton went in wildly for peace; and instead of putting himself on the defensive, YIKSHAN went in wildly for war: whilst, again, YEN PEH-T'AO, YÜK'IEN, and NIU KIEN went in for wildly defending indefensible places. If they had only known how to take advantage of the ground, guard the inner waters, strengthen their fortifications, drill their best troops, prepare a store of combustibles, and lay a series of ambushes, like LIN and TÊNG did at the Bogue and Amoy! They should have appeared unable to conquer, and then waited to see if the enemy could give them the opportunity to conquer; when they could have fought on the defensive, or remained on the defensive whilst treating. If they had fought on the defensive, they would have had the benefit of other troops besides our own;—for instance, the French and Americans, and also the Ghoorkas, as far as setting foreign enemy against foreign enemy goes: and they would have had the benefit of other Chinese besides the patriots;—for instance, our rapscallions, as far as setting disloyalists against the enemy goes. If, on the other hand, they had remained on the defensive whilst treating, then we should have had nothing to fear, whilst they would have had everything to ask. We should have resolutely adhered to the opium interdiction as a means of closing their mouths and taking the spirit out of them, leaving the other barbarians deprived of their trade to come in as mediators, in which condition we could never but be declared by the latter otherwise than in the right against the English; whilst we must have gained their affection in the same measure as the English their hatred. In this way not only should we not have had to pay for any opium, but we should have been able to prevent for ever its coming any more in the future; whilst the millions of money which we had to spend in war indemnities to the barbarians could have been devoted to the purchase of foreign guns and ships, the training of marines and firemen to attack, etc.; thus appropriating to our own purposes the armaments and defences of the foreigners themselves, and turning their arts and devices into *our* arts and devices, and at one effort both enriching the state and strengthening our arms.

Oh! opportunity! opportunity! It is only the true genius who can take opportunity by the forelock! It is only the sagacious who never *miss* opportunity. But the next best thing is to repent when the opportunity has gone by. Repentance, followed by capacity to change for the better, will yet enable us to repair our errors at some future time!

KELLY & WALSH, LIMITED, PRINTERS, SHANGHAI.

IN THE PRESS:

By the same Author:

"CHINESE ACCOUNT OF EUROPEANS, THEIR RELIGIONS, COMMERCE, AND WARS."

CORRIGENDA.

Page 4, for 池　　　　read 地.

,, 7 ,, [Madras]^d ,, Mêng-mai [Bombay]^d

,, 11 ,, our favour ,, Our favour.

,, 37 ,, you succeeded ,, you have succeeded.

,, 62 ,, fleet had to ,, fleet had had to.

,, 81 ,, never but be ,, never be.

The Pagoda Library.　　　　　　　　　No. 1.

Chinese Account

OF THE

Opium War.

1888.　　　　　　　　　E. H. PARKER.

CHINESE ACCOUNT

OF THE

OPIUM WAR.

The Pagoda Library.　　　　No. 1.

Chinese Account

of the

Opium War.

1888.　　　By E. H. PARKER.

Chinese Account

of the

Opium War.

BY

E. H. PARKER.

Shanghai:
KELLY & WALSH, LIMITED,
SHANGHAI—HONGKONG—YOKOHAMA—SINGAPORE.

1888.

PREFACE.

THE following story of the Opium War is to all intents and purposes a translation of the last two chapters of the *Shêng Wu-ki*, or "Military Operations of the present Dynasty." The author is WEI YÜAN, a Chinese who held, about forty years ago, the post of Department Magistrate at Kao-yu, north of Yangchow; and WEI YÜAN's style has been followed in the translation. Dates have been altered so as to convey definite ideas of time to European readers, and in some cases the Cantonese or other popular pronunciation is given to the names of places and persons well known in the south. In some parts the original is digested, and wearisome portions have been omitted.

The paper illustrates the extraordinary faithfulness with which the Chinese endeavour to perfect their histories; and this seems to have always been a national characteristic. In the work of solving the riddles of ancient and mediæval history, the Chinese records (if correctly translated) are likely to be found as faithful as any, though there may be mistakes.

E. H. PARKER.

Printed in Great Britain
by Amazon